D1189607

WITHDRAWN

THE YALE SERIES OF YOUNGER POETS

Edited by Stephen Vincent Benét

THEORY OF FLIGHT

London · Humphrey Milford · Oxford University Press

THEORY OF FLIGHT

BY MURIEL RUKEYSER

WITH A FOREWORD BY STEPHEN VINCENT BENÉT

NEW HAVEN · YALE UNIVERSITY PRESS

PS
3535
U4
T5
1935

Copyright, 1935, by Yale University Press

Printed in the United States of America

First published, November, 1935
Second printing, February, 1936
Third printing, September, 1939

All rights reserved. This book may not be reproduced, in whole or in part, in any form (except by reviewers for the public press), without written permission from the publishers.

I wish here to thank Horace and Marya Gregory, Nancy Naumburg, Stephen Vincent Benét, Elizabeth Ames, Henry Fuller, Flora Rosenmeyer, and my parents, Lawrence and Myra Rukeyser.

Some of these poems have appeared in Poetry, Dynamo, New Republic, New Masses, Herald-Tribune Books, The Magazine, Partisan Review, Housatonic, Trend, Vassar Review, Trial Balances, Student Outlook, Con Spirito, Kosmos, Alcestis, Student Review, Smoke, and Westminster Review.

FOREWORD

Some people are born with their craft already in their hand, and, from her first book, Miss Rukeyser seems to be one of these. There is little of the uncertainty, the fumbling, the innocently direct imitation of admirations which one unconsciously associates with a first book of verse. It is, some of it, work in a method, but the method is handled maturely and the occasional uncertainties are rather from experimentation than any technical insufficiency. Moreover, there is a great deal of power—a remarkable power for twenty-one. I don't know quite what Miss Rukeyser will do with the future but she certainly will be a writer. It sticks out all over the book.

Politically, she is a Left Winger and a revolutionary. She speaks for her part of the generation born "in Prinzip's year" that found the world they grew up in too bitterly tainted by that year to accept.

> "We focus on our times, destroying you, fathers
> in the long ground—you have given strange birth
> to us who turn against you in our blood."

she says in "The Blood Is Justified" and again

> "I do not say   :   Forgive, to my kindred dead,
>   only   :   Understand my treason, See I betray you kissing,
> I overthrow your milestones weeping among your tombs."

I do not intend to add, in this preface, to the dreary and unreal discussion about unconscious fascists, conscious proletarians, and other figures of straw which has afflicted recent criticism with head noises and small specks in front of the eyes. But I will remark that when Miss Rukeyser speaks her politics— and she speaks with sincerity and fire—she does so like a poet, not like a slightly worn phonograph record, and she does so in poetic terms. For evidence, I offer the section "The Lynchings of Jesus" in the long poem "Theory of Flight"; the short "shot" of the coal-mine in the elegy for Ruth Lehman and the poem "The Blood Is Justified," among others. They are worth reading, to see what a young and talented person thinks of certain contemporary things—and how a poet of talent can make poetry out of them.

I use the word "shot" advisedly—for the mind behind these poems is an urban and a modern one. It has fed on the quick jerk of the news-reel, the hard lights in the sky, the long deserted night-street, the take-off of the plane from the ground. It knows nature as well—the look of landscape, the quietness of hills. But its experience has been largely an urban experience, and it is interesting to see the poetry of youth so based. When Miss Rukeyser thinks of energy, she thinks of a dynamo rather than a river, an electric spark rather than a trampling hoof—and that is interesting, too.

Perhaps that makes her verse sound like verse of the "Oh, Grandmother

Dynamo, what great big wheels you have!" school—and that, most decidedly, it is not. Witness "Song for Dead Children," "Breathing Landscape," and the beautiful and original "Thousands of Days," with its serene and successful assonance. She can write powerfully; she can also write delicately, to a new and light-footed pattern. Her technique is sure, and is developing in original directions. Her long poem, "Theory of Flight," is a rather unusual achievement for a girl in her twenties. It has passages of confusion and journalistic passages, it also has passages that remind one of structural steel. There is a largeness of attempt about it which is one of the surest signs of genuine ability. Her later lyrics, particularly the ones I have mentioned, are more successfully and surely integrated. But only an original mind could have accomplished both.

Miss Rukeyser is twenty-one. She was born and brought up in New York City and has attended Vassar, the Columbia Summer School, and the Roosevelt School of the Air (the latter to gather material for "Theory of Flight"). At present, she is on the staff of "New Theatre." I think we may expect a good deal from her in the future. And it would seem to me that in this first book she displays an accomplishment which ranks her among the most interesting and individual of our younger poets.

Stephen Vincent Benét

CONTENTS

III. The Blood Is Justified

POEM OUT OF CHILDHOOD

POEM OUT OF CHILDHOOD

I

Breathe-in experience, breathe-out poetry　:
Not Angles, angels　:　and the magnificent past
shot deep illuminations into high-school.
I opened the door into the concert-hall
and a rush of triumphant violins answered me
while the syphilitic woman turned her mouldered face
intruding upon Brahms.　　Suddenly, in an accident
the girl's brother was killed, but her father had just died　:
she stood against the wall, leaning her cheek,
dumbly her arms fell, "What will become of me?" and
I went into the corridor for a drink of water.
These bandages of image wrap my head
when I put my hand up I hardly feel the wounds.
We sat on the steps of the unrented house
raining blood down on Loeb and Leopold,
creating again how they removed his glasses
and philosophically slit his throat.

　　They who manipulated and misused our youth,
　　smearing those centuries upon our hands,
　　trapping us in a welter of dead names,
　　snuffing and shaking heads at patent truth. . . .

We were ready to go the long descent with Virgil
the bough's gold shade advancing forever with us,
entering the populated cold of drawing-rooms;
Sappho, with her drowned hair trailing along Greek waters,
weed binding it, a fillet of kelp enclosing
the temples' ardent fruit　:

　　　　　　Not Sappho, Sacco.
Rebellion pioneered among our lives,
viewing from far-off many-branching deltas,
innumerable seas.

SALEM COLLEGE LIBRARY
Winston-Salem, North Carolina

II

In adolescence I knew travellers
speakers digressing from the ink-pocked rooms,
bearing the unequivocal sunny word.

Prinzip's year bore us :   see us turning at breast
quietly while the air throbs over Sarajevo
after the mechanic laugh of that bullet.
How could they know what sinister knowledge finds
its way among our brains' wet palpitance,
what words would nudge and giggle at our spine,
what murders dance?
These horrors have approached the growing child;
now that the factory is sealed-up brick
the kids throw stones, smashing the windows,
membranes of uselessness in desolation.

We grew older quickly, watching the father shave
and the splatter of lather hardening on the glass,
playing in sandboxes to escape paralysis,
being victimized by fataller sly things.
"Oh, and you," he said, scraping his jaw, "what will you be?"
"Maybe : something : like : Joan : of : Arc. . . ."
Allies Advance, we see,
Six Miles South to Soissons.   And we beat the drums.
Watchsprings snap in the mind, uncoil, relax,
the leafy years all somber with foreign war.
How could we know what exposed guts resembled?

A wave, shocked to motion, babbles margins
from Asia to Far Rockaway spiralling
among clocks in its four-dimensional circles.
Disturbed by war we pedalled bicycles
breakneck down the decline, until the treads .
conquered our speed and pulled our feet behind them,
and pulled our heads.
We never knew the war, standing so small
looking at eye-level toward the puttees, searching
the picture-books for sceptres, pennants for truth;
see Galahad unaided by puberty.

Ratat a drum upon the armistice,
Kodak As You Go :   photo :   they danced late,
and we were a generation of grim children
leaning over the bedroom sills, watching
the music and the shoulders and how the war was over,
laughing until the blow on the mouth broke night
wide out from cover.
The child's curls blow in a forgotten wind,
immortal ivy trembles on the wall:
the sun has crystallized these scenes, and tall
shadows remember time cannot rescind.

III

Organize the full results of that rich past
open the windows   :   potent catalyst,
harsh theory of knowledge, running down the aisles
crying out in the classrooms, March ravening on the plain,
inexorable sun and wind and natural thought.
Dialectically our youth unfolds   :
the pale child walking to the river, passional
in ignorance   in loneliness   demanding
its habitation for the leaping dream, kissing
quick air, the vibrations of transient light,
not knowing substance or reserve, walking
in valvular air, each person in the street
conceived surrounded by his life and pain,
fixed against time, subtly by these impaled   :
death and that shapeless war.   Listening at dead doors,
our youth assumes a thousand differing flesh
summoning fact from abandoned machines of trade,
knocking on the wall of the nailed-up power-plant,
telephoning hello, the deserted factory, ready
for the affirmative clap of truth
ricochetting from thought to thought among
the childhood, the gestures, the rigid travellers.

SONG FOR DEAD CHILDREN

We set great wreaths of brightness on the graves of the passionate
who required tribute of hot July flowers   :
for you, O brittle-hearted, we bring offering
remembering how your wrists were thin and your delicate bones
        not yet braced for conquering.

The sharp cries of ghost-boys are keen above the meadows,
the little girls continue graceful and wondering;
flickering evening on the lakes recalls those young
heirs whose developing years have sunk to earth
        their strength not tested, their praise unsung.

Weave grasses for their childhood   :   who will never see
love or disaster or take sides against decay
balancing the choices of maturity;
silent and coffin'd in silence while we pass
        loud in defiance of death, the helpless lie.

I N   A   D A R K   H O U S E

Two on the stairs in a house where they had loved   :
mounting, and the steps a long ascent before them
brown: a single step creaking high in the flight; the turn   :
the quiet house and the cheese-yellow walls shadowed by night,
dark; and the unlit lamps along the wall.
Dusk piles in old house-corners rapidly.   Shade grows
where corners round to flights of stairs again.   Evening
accumulates under the treads of mounting stairs.
They rise: he tightly-knit, clenched in anxiety, she calm,
massive in female beauty, precise line of brow
curving to generous cheek and mouth and throat,
and his face bright and strained with eagerness.

But the nights are restless with these dreams of ours
in which we cry, fling our arms abroad, and there is no one;
walls close in to a shaft and blur of brown:
out of the chaos and eclipse of mind rise stairs.
(Here, metrically and monotonously walks
each several person unprotectedly.)
Alone, the nightmare broadens in the rising,
dull step sinking behind dull step, now, here, here,
nothing in the world but the slow spiral rise, expectancy, and fear.

He turns his face to her, walk unbroken.   Her face
questioning turns: there is no help for each
in the other.   There are no eyes on them.   The shaft
is empty of voices, all but the creaking step, regularly
in the flights recurring, preknown, dreaded that sound.
There is no face that he can see but hers.
She knows his look, and has known it for a long time.
The creak of the one step is a punctuating rhyme.

But the nights are restless with receding faces
in massed battalions through the solemn air,
vivid with brightness, clangorous with sounds:
struck copper, chiming cylinders of silver, horns   :

presences in the outer air.   But here
only the empty shaft and the painful stairs.

He remembers the men and women he has loved:
fine-curved and brittle skulls housing strange ardency,
the male hard bravery of argument   :
lips of women, love-writhen, and their hands,
pale fruit of comfort, pliant, governing, white consolation
against small fear and human bodily pain,
never against the terror of the stairs.

Remembrances of words, human counsel in sounds, and pictures,
books, and the bleak rush of shining towers,
tunes crop through the tired brain: Ravel's "Bolero,"
an old blues going "Love, Oh Love, Oh Loveless Love,"
humping through air powerfully with its sound.

She remembers the men and women she has loved:
the full soft cheeks of girls, their secrecies,
grave words that fell with sweet continuance in her youth   :
men's eyes, dumb with meaning unspeakable and low-sounding
among the intricate memories deep in her recessed mind,
the length of their arms, the firm triangled backs, stalwart,
turning beautifully in their planes on the narrow hips,
dark ease beneath their arms and eyes, strength in their voices,
but ebbing away in the silence of the stairs.

Remembrances of wind shaking November evenings,
arpeggioed skyscrapers, clean-heavy-falling waters   :
"There's No Today, There's No Tomorrow"
debates against a symphony of Brahms',
and foot follows foot heavily in the row.

He had gone to play apart, by the hollows of the sand
cupped (a pale arm about the ocean's blue)   :
picked pebbles and the soft-voluted shells,
laver and dulse, dark flowers of the sea.
He had been a child in a fantastic wood
where the dim statues stood, posturing gothically,
and "Mother, mother, mother!" cried   :   but they
remained with closed lips ceremonially.
The ocean and his mother and his childhood let him be

until he had grown and finished his lessons and his prayers,
and then   :   these stairs.

Night is treacherous with dreams betraying us,
leaving us vulnerable to inherited shame,
crying out against our secret, naming an occult name.

And she had enjoyed narrow fields, shaven lawns,
tiny stones freckled brown and white and red,
green water troubled by waves of a twig's making,
grown out of these to wider thoughts that bred
high spaces and new knowledges, and cared for some
with mind and body, some with love only of eyes and head.
She had believed in the quick response to pain,
in union of crowds living in one belief,
a social order kept by a coöperative strain
steadily toward one thing, but aware of all   :
she had reached out her hand with the gesture of one who dares,
and found   :   these stairs.

The stairs still rise.   The halls remain, and dull
and somber stand to be trodden by the quiet two rising
laboriously along the fateful road.   They should be high now.
(If the dun walls should slide into the night,
faces might be disclosed, bitter, impotent, angered
above slant shoulders swinging toolless arms, great hands
jointed around no implements, and the silent mouths
opened to cry for law.   Some faces black, the rope
knotted beneath an ear, some black with the strong blood
of Negroes, some yellow and concentrate, all fixed
on the tower of stairs, should the walls sink, perhaps
all waiting, perhaps nothing but unanswering dark.)
They must be high.   There are no voices.   The shaft is very still.

Night is sick with our dreams.   Night is florid
with our by-reason-uncontested imagings.   We in our time
(not we   :   you   :   in your time   :   no credit ours)
have built brave stone on stone, and called their blazonry
*Beauty Old Yet Ever New   :   Eternal Voice
And Inward Word   :   (a blur of fond noises signifying

* New York Public Library.

a long thing) and raised signs, saying:
*But Of All Things Truth Beareth Away
The Victory   :   (the pock-bitten pass to spit
gelatinously and obscenely on the bird-marked stones,
and shallow-carven letters fade).   The evil night
of our schooled minds is morbid with our dreams.

Whir.   Whirl of brown stairs.   Cool brow.   Athenian lips.
The creaking stairs.   Stupid   stupid   stupidly   stupidly
we go a long voyage on the stairs of a house
builded on stairs.   One stair creaks forever amen in the Name.
Treads rock under the feet.   The two go   :   he tight and harsh
(but limp with warm exhaustion), she plods   :   one, two, foot   :   on
up   mounting   up   O lovely stairs, hideous and cruel
we propitiate you with incensuous words   stairs   lovely   loved
rise, idol of our walking days and nights,
travelled-forever road of the lordly mind   :   with shaking bannisters
and no sound crawling through the wall-hole-lips   :
love-writhen women's lips   :   the crackled lips of the mass
that must be there waiting for law at the wall's decay.
Large female   :   male   :   come tiredness and sleep
come peace   come generous power over no other, come Order here.
Steps mount.   The brown treads rise.   Stairs.   Rise up.   Stairs.

* New York Public Library.

EFFORT AT SPEECH
BETWEEN TWO PEOPLE

:   Speak to me.   Take my hand.   What are you now?
I will tell you all.   I will conceal nothing.
When I was three, a little child read a story about a rabbit
who died, in the story, and I crawled under a chair   :
a pink rabbit   :   it was my birthday, and a candle
burnt a sore spot on my finger, and I was told to be happy.

:   Oh, grow to know me.   I am not happy.   I will be open:
Now I am thinking of white sails against a sky like music,
like glad horns blowing, and birds tilting, and an arm about me.
There was one I loved, who wanted to live, sailing.

:   Speak to me.   Take my hand.   What are you now?
When I was nine, I was fruitily sentimental,
fluid   :   and my widowed aunt played Chopin,
and I bent my head on the painted woodwork, and wept.
I want now to be close to you.   I would
link the minutes of my days close, somehow, to your days.

:   I am not happy.   I will be open.
I have liked lamps in evening corners, and quiet poems.
There has been fear in my life.   Sometimes I speculate
On what a tragedy his life was, really.

:   Take my hand.   Fist my mind in your hand.   What are you now?
When I was fourteen, I had dreams of suicide,
and I stood at a steep window, at sunset, hoping toward death   :
if the light had not melted clouds and plains to beauty,
if light had not transformed that day, I would have leapt.
I am unhappy.   I am lonely.   Speak to me.

:   I will be open.   I think he never loved me:
he loved the bright beaches, the little lips of foam
that ride small waves, he loved the veer of gulls:
he said with a gay mouth: I love you.   Grow to know me.

:   What are you now?   If we could touch one another,
if these our separate entities could come to grips,
clenched like a Chinese puzzle . . . yesterday
I stood in a crowded street that was live with people,
and no one spoke a word, and the morning shone.
Everyone silent, moving. . . . Take my hand.   Speak to me.

NOTES FOR A POEM

Here are the long fields inviolate of thought,
here are the planted fields raking the sky,
signs in the earth   :
water-cast shuttles of light flickering the underside of rock.
These have been shown before; but the fields know new hands,
the son's fingers grasp warmly at the father's hoe   ;
there will be new ways of seeing these ancestral lands.

    "In town, the munitions plant has been poor since the war,
      And nothing but a war will make it rich again."
    Holy, holy, holy, sings the church next door.

Time-ridden, a man strides the current of a stream's flowing,
stands, flexing the wand curvingly over his head,
tracking the water's prism with the flung line.
Summer becomes productive and mature.
Farmers watch tools like spikes of doom against the sure
condemning sky descending upon the hollow lands.

    The water is ridged in muscles on the rock,
    force for the State is planted in the stream-bed.
    Water springs from the stone   —   the State is fed.

Morning comes, brisk with light,
a broom of color over the threshold.
Long flights of shadows escape to the white sky   :
a spoon is straightened.   Day grows.   The sky is blued.

    The water rushes over the shelves of stone
    to anti-climax on the mills below the drop.
    The planted fields are bright and rake the sky.
    Power is common.   Earth is grown
    and overgrown in unrelated strength, the moral
    rehearsed already, often.
    (There must be the gearing of these facts
    into coördination, in a poem or numbers,

rows of statistics, or the cool iambs.)
The locked relationships which will be found
are a design to build these factual timbers—
a plough of thought to break this stubborn ground.

P L A C E – R I T U A L S

T R A D I T I O N   O F   T H I S   A C R E

This is the word our lips caress, our teeth bite
on the pale spongy fruit of this, the name   :
mouthing the story, cowlike in dignity, and spitting it
in the tarnished cuspidor of present days.
And if there were radium in Plymouth Rock, they would not strike it
 (bruising the fair stone), nor gawk at Semiramis on Main Street
nor measure the gentle Christ in terms of horse-power.
Cracked bells are severally struck at noon.
The furrow of their ways will cradle us all.
Amen, amen, to the ritual of our habit, fall
before the repetitions in the lips of doom.

R I T U A L   O F   B L E S S I N G

The proud colors and brittle cloths, the supple smoke rising,
the metal symbols precious to our dreams
loftily borne.   **Thy Kingdom come.**
                        We have blessed the fields with speech.
There are alp-passes in the travelled mind
(they have stood in the quiet air, making signs on the sky
to bless the cities of the shining plain).
The climate of the mind is the warmth of a shrine
and the air torn with incense.   **World without end.**
How can we bless this place   :   by the sweet horns,
the vaulted words, the pastoral lovers in the waist-deep grass,
remembrances linking back, hands raised like strict flames pointing,
the feet of priests tracking the smooth earth,
many hands binding corn   :   ?   **Thy Kingdom come.**
There are pale steeples erect among the green,
blood falling before the eyes of love   the lids fire-bright,
hands together in the fields, the born and unborn children,
and the wish for new blessing and the given blessing blend,
a glory clear in the man-tracks, in the blind
seeking for warmth in the climates of the mind.
                        World without end.
                                Amen.

WOODEN SPRING

How horrible late spring is, with the full death of the frozen tight bulbs
brownly rotting in earth; and each chord of light
rayed into slivers, a bunch of grapes plucked grape by grape apart,
a warm chord broken into the chilled single notes.

(Let us rely on cerebral titillation
for the red stimulus of sensuous supply;)
here is no heat, no fierce color: spring is no bacchante this year
eager to celebrate her carnal dedication.

The ghosts swim, lipless, eyeless, upward   :
the crazy hands point in five directions down   :
to the sea, the high ridge, the bush, the blade, the weak white root   :
thumping at life in an agony of birth, abortive fruit.

Spring is very mad for greenness now
(:   I suppose it would be beautiful, if we let ourselves be   :   ),
but we must strip nascent earth bare of green mystery.
Trees do not grow high as skyscrapers in my town,

and flowers not so lovely as the pale bewildered youth,
hands pointing in five directions upward and out;
and spring in the fields and cities spreads to the north and south,
and is comforted in desire for the sun's mouth.

Earth does not seem wooden to the comforted spring   :
(spring could not seem so dull, I comforted   :
but there must be abstraction, where fields need not sprout, waves pound,
there must be silence where no rushing grasses sound,
life in this lack of death, comfort on this wide ground).

SONNET

My thoughts through yours refracted into speech
transmute this room musically tonight,
the notes of contact flowing, rhythmic, bright
with an informal art beyond my single reach.
Outside, dark birds fly in a greening time   :
wings of our sistered wishes beat these walls   :
and words afflict our minds in near footfalls
approaching with a latening hour's chime.

And if an essential thing has flown between us,
rare intellectual bird of communication,
let us seize it quickly   ;   let our preference
choose it instead of softer things to screen us
each from the other's self   :   muteness or hesitation,
nor petrify live miracle by our indifference.

unity, harmony, variety & contrast, rhythm, balance & proportion

LETTER, UNPOSTED

"My love, my love, my love, why have you left me alone?"

James Joyce

If I could write : Summer waits your coming,
the flowers are colored, but half-alive and weak,
earth sickens, as I sicken, with waiting,
and the clouds print on the dull moon a dark and blotting streak.
If I could write : no energy is kinetic,
storm breaks nor foot falls until you arrive,
the trees thrive, but no fruit is born to hang
heavily : and the stale wind continues to drive
all pausing summer before it into the distance
from which you, shining, will come. . . . But summer lives,
and minds grow, and nerves are sensitized to power
and no winds wait, and no tree stands but gives
richly to the store of the burning harvest :
the door stands open for you, and other figures pass,
and I receive them joyfully and live : but wait for you
(and sometimes secretly watch for wrinkles, in my glass).

SAND – QUARRY WITH
MOVING FIGURES

Father and I drove to the sand-quarry across the ruined marshlands,
miles of black grass, burned for next summer's green.
I reached my hand to his beneath the lap-robe,
we looked at the stripe of fire, the blasted scene.

"It's all right," he said, "they can control the flames,
on one side men are standing, and on the other the sea;"
but I was terrified of stubble and waste of black
and his ugly villages he built and was showing me.

The countryside turned right and left about the car,
straight through October we drove to the pit's heart;
sand, and its yellow canyon and standing pools
and the wealth of the split country set us farther apart.
"Look," he said, "this quarry means rows of little houses,
stucco and a new bracelet for you are buried there;"
but I remembered the ruined patches, and I saw the land ruined,
exploded, burned away, and the fiery marshes bare.

"We'll own the countryside, you'll see how soon I will,
you'll have acres to play in"   :   I saw the written name
painted on stone in the face of the steep hill:
"That's your name, Father!"   "And yours!" he shouted, laughing.
"No, Father, no!"   He caught my hand as I cried,
and smiling, entered the pit, ran laughing down its side.

WEDDING PRESENTS

I

Griefs
marking indelibly our later loves.

Fantastic juxtapose that sets the wish
opposite the insubordinate flesh
interring the fact of the inconstant rain
in the fixed lightly-palpitant brain,

the anthropoid hunger laid against the will
making small music in the ventricle
until evolved man hears with each breath-intake
the sweetly mathematical sound of Bach.

II

Be bold, friend   ;   all your nymphs have disappeared
dwindled upon those green and classic banks,
the goddesses are gone, and the chivalric ranks.
Where'er you walk, cool gales will fan the glade
breathing themselves to death, sighing against the towers
upon the firm and beautiful machines   ;
trees, where you sit, will crowd into a shade
eclipsing Handel, shining electric powers
of energy on polytechnic scenes.
Believe Eurydice unregained at last,
see that those idyll afternoons are past.
Accept the gathering skies that tell our morning,
open your hands   open your thighs   for strength
inviolate in beauty, ill-defined
ready for the Columbus of the mind.

Trembling, the mouth relaxes in the kiss.
The lemon body and purple blood beneath
award themselves in love, most perfect wreath.

THREE SIDES OF A COIN

I

Am I in your light?
           No, go on reading
    (the hackneyed light of evening quarrelling with the bulbs;
      the book's bent rectangle solid on your knees)
only my fingers in your hair, only, my eyes
splitting the skull to tickle your brain with love
in a slow caress blurring the mind,
                  kissing your mouth awake
opening the body's mouth and stopping the words.
This light is thick with birds, and
evening warns us beautifully of death.
Slowly I bend over you, slowly your breath
runs rhythms through my blood
as if I said
            I love you
and you should raise your head
listening, speaking into the covert night
   : Did someone say something?
             Love, am I in your light?
Am I?

Refrain See how love alters the living face
           go spin the immortal coin through time
           watch the thing flip through space
               tick   tick

II

We all had a good time
              the throne was there and all
and there she was with that primitive unforgivable mouth
saying sophistications about nothing at all
as the young men cavorted up the room Darling
it's a swell party and those Martinis with

the olives so delicately soaked in alcohol
        and William Flesh, the inventor, being cute
about the revolution and the Negro Question
until Dick said "Lynch the Jews!" (his name was Fleischman
but the war brought about a number of changes)
and the Objectivist poet fresh from Butte
with his prePosterous suggestion. . . .
        After a while, of course, we left,
the room was getting so jammed with editors.
And William and Maurice and Del and I
went back and we took turns using the couch with them.
        We all had a good time
and Del had hysterics at about 3 A. M.
        we dashed water into her face
        I held her temples and Maurice said
        what could we hope to look for next:
        it's one thing to be faithful to the dead
        (he said) but for her to stick to an oversexed
old fool   :   but she only laughed and cried and beat the floor
until the neighbors rattled at the door.

Refrain   Runnels of wine ran down his chin and laughter
            softened his words until quite suddenly
            the walls fell and the night stood blank and after
                    tick   tick

III

He turned the lights on and walked to the window   :
Son of a bitch   :   he said   :   if it isn't the reds again
parading through the streets with those lousy posters.
The Village was never like this in the old days,
throw a brick down the street and you'd hit a female poet
and life went on like a string of roller coasters.

                Workers of the world   :
we've worked the world for all the damn thing's worth
                tick   tick
I was little and they promised me the hills of glory
a great life and a sounding name on the earth   :
                tick   tick
            this is a different story.

Here's a list I've been making   :   reasons for living
on the right, reasons for my sudden death on the left.
Right now they balance so I could flip a coin
determine the imperative tonight
                tick   tick
flip that amazing coin through time and space this night
and the Village   :   and the army with banners
                     and the hot girls
and the rotgut all gone
                   like a blown fuse   :
I'd get a paragraph or two of news
obituary as a shutting door
meaning no more
           leaving the world to the sun and the workers
           the straight beautiful children   the coins   the clocks
                  tick   tick

BREATHING LANDSCAPE

Lying in the sun
and lying here so still
an egg might slowly hatch in this still hand.

The people pass
abruptly they nod   :   they smile
trailed in the air, silence follows their faces.

I know, lying
how the hills are fixed
and the day-moon runs at the head of the fixed hills.

Nothing crossed the field
all day but a bird
skirting the tall grass in briefest transit.

Their stern ideas
are a long work to each
and even armored we hardly touch each other.

The wind leans,
the air placed formally
about these faces and thoughts in formal dance.

Silence hangs in the air.
Nothing speaks but the sound
of certain rivers continuing underground.

F O U R   I N   A   F A M I L Y

The father and mother sat, and the sister beside her.
I faced the two women across the table's width,
speaking, and all the time he looked at me,
sorrowing, saying nothing, with his hard tired breath.

Their faces said   :   This is your home; and I   :
I never come home, I never go away.
And they all answered   :   Stay.

All day the city turned about this room,
and silence had remained between our faces,
divisions outside to concentrate a world
tally here only to dead profits and losses.

We follow barrier voices, and we go fast,
unknown to each other, they race, I turn away.
No voice is strong enough to cry me Stay.

 My sister, I wished upon you those delights
 time never buries,
 more precious than heroes.

 Strange father, strange mother, who are you, who are you?
 Where have I come,
 how shall I prosper home?

THIS HOUSE, THIS COUNTRY

Always I travelled farther
dreading a barrier
starting at shadows scattered on the ground
fearful of the invisible night-sound,

till in that straight career
I crossed frontier
the questions asked   the proofs shown   the name
signed smiling   I reached knowledge of my home.

I praised their matings
and corner-meetings
their streets the brightest I had yet walked down   :
my family swore I did not leave my town

thought that I lied
and had not signed
those passports, tickets, contracts, bills of sale
but still rested among them and wished them well.

Over my shoulder
I see they grow older
their vision fails   :   observe I travel light
fear distance   hope I shall only spend the night.

But night in this country
is deep promise of day,
is busy with preparations and awake for fighting
and there is no time for leavetaking and regretting.

I know their tired house
full of remorse
I know in my body the door, the entrance-hall
a wall and my space and another wall.

I have left forever
house and maternal river
given up sitting in that private tomb
quitted that land   that house   that velvet room.

Frontiers admitted me
to a growing country
I carry the proofs of my birth and my mind's reasons
but reckon with their struggle and their seasons.

THEORY OF FLIGHT

PREAMBLE

Earth, bind us close, and time   ;   nor, sky, deride
how violate we experiment again.
In many Januaries, many lips
have fastened on us while we deified
the waning flesh   :   now, fountain, spout for us,
mother, bear children   :   lover, yet once more   :
in final effort toward your mastery.
Many Decembers suffered their eclipse
death, and forgetfulness, and the year bore round   ;
now years, be summed in one access of power.
Fortresses, strengths, beauties, realities,
gather together, discover to us our wings
new special product of mortality.

Fortuitously have we gained loneliness,
fallen in waste places liberated,
relieved ourselves from weakness' loveliness   :
remain unpitied now, never descend
to that soft howling of the prostrate mind.
Cut with your certain wings;   engrave space now
to your ambition   :   stake off sky's dimensions.
We have plunged on nightmares to destruction
too long; and learned aggression divides wind,
pale early Venus is signature of night
and wish gnawed clean by plans precurses flight.
Distinguish the metaphor most chromium clear
for distant calendars to identify   :
Frail mouthings will fall diminished on old ears
in dusty whispers, light from extinctest stars
will let us sleep, nor may we replica
ourselves in hieroglyphs and broken things
but there is reproduction for this act
linking the flight's escape with strict contact.

.   .   .   .   .

Look! Be : leap ;
paint trees in flame
bushes burning
roar in the broad sky
know your color : be :
produce that the widenesses
be full and burst their wombs
riot in redness, delirious with light,
swim bluely through the mind
shout green as the day breaks
put up your face to the wind
FLY

chant as the tomtom hubbubs crash
elephants in the flesh's jungle
reek with vigor   sweat   pour your life
in a libation to itself
drink from the ripe ground
make children over the world
lust in a heat of tropic orange
stamp and writhe ; stamp on a wet floor
know earth   know water   know lovers
know mastery
FLY

   . . . . .

  Walks down the street
  Kaleidoscope   a man
  where patterns meet
  his mind colored
  with mirage
  Leonardo's tomb
  not in Italian earth
  but in a fuselage
  designed
  in the historic mind
  time's instrument
  blue-print of birth.

   . . . . .

We know sky overhead, earth to be stepped
black under the toes, rubble between our fingers,

horizons are familiar   ;   we have been taught colors.
Rehearse these   ;   sky, earth, and their meeting-place,
confound them in a blur of distance, swallow
the blueness of guessed-at places, merge them now.
Sky being meeting of sky and no-sky
including our sources   the earth   water   air
fire to weld them   :   unity in knowing
all space in one unpunctuated flowing.
Flight, thus, is meeting of flight and no-flight.
We bear the seeds of our return forever,
the flowers of our leaving, fruit of flight,
perfect for present, fertile for its roots
in past   in future   in motility.

THE GYROSCOPE

But this is our desire, and of its worth. . . .
Power electric-clean, gravitating outward at all points,
moving in savage fire, fusing all durable stuff
but never itself being fused with any force
homing in no hand nor breast nor sex
for buried in these lips we rise again,
bent over these plans, our faces raise to see.
Direct spears are shot outward from the conscience
fulfilling what far circuits?   Orbit of thought
what axis do you lean on, what strictnesses evade
impelled to the long curves of the will's ambition?
Centrifugal power, expanding universe
within expanding universe, what stillnesses
lie at your center resting among motion?
Study communications, looking inward, find what traffic
you may have with your silences   :   looking outward, survey
what you have seen of places   :
                                    many times this week I seemed
          to hear you speak my name
                              how you turn the flatnesses
          of your cheek and will not hear my words
                              then reaching the given latitude
          and longitude, we searched for the ship and found nothing
                              and, gentlemen, shall we define desire
          including every impulse toward psychic progress?
Roads are cut into the earth leading away from our place
at the inevitable hub.   All directions are **out,**
all desire turns outward   :   we, introspective,
continuing to find in ourselves the microcosm
imaging continents, powers, relations, reflecting
all history in a bifurcated Engine.
Here is the gyroscope whirling out pulsing in tides illimitably
                    widening, live force contained
in a sphere of rigid boundary   ;   concentrate
at the locus of all forces, spinning with black speed
revolving outward perpetually, turning with its torque

all the developments of the secret will.
Flaming origins were our fathers in the heat of the earth,
pushing to the crust, water and sea-flesh,
undulant tentacles ingrown on the ocean's floor,
frondy anemones and scales' armor gave us birth.
Bring us to air, ancestors! and we breathed
the young flesh wincing against naked December.
Masters of fire, fire gave us riches, gave us life.
Masters of water, water gave us riches, gave us life,
masters of earth, earth gave us riches, gave us life.
Air mocks, and desire whirls outward in strict frenzy, leaping,
elastic circles widening from the mind,
turning constricted to the mind again.
The dynamics of desire are explained
in terms of action outward and reaction to a core
obscured and undefined, except, perhaps, as "God in Heaven," "God in Man,"
Elohim intermittent with the soul, recurrent
as Father and Holy Ghost, Word and responsive Word,
merging with contact in continual sunbursts,
the promise, the response, the hands laid on,
the hammer swung to the anvil, mouth fallen on mouth,
the plane nose up into an open sky.
Roads are cut, purchase is gained on our wish,
the turbines gather momentum, tools are given   :
whirl in desire, hurry to ambition, return,
maintaining the soul's polarity   ;   be   :   fly.

THE LYNCHINGS OF JESUS

I. PASSAGE TO GODHEAD

Passage to godhead, fitfully glared upon
by bloody shinings over Calvary
this latest effort to revolution stabbed
against a bitter crucificial tree,
mild thighs split by the spearwound, opening
in fierce gestation of immortality.

Icarus' phoenix-flight fulfils itself,
desire's symbol swings full circle here,
eternal defeat by power, eternal death
of the soul and body in murder or despair
to be followed by eternal return, until
the thoughtful rebel may triumph everywhere.

Many murdered in war, crucified, starved,
loving their lives they are massacred and burned,
hating their lives as they have found them, but
killed while they look to enjoy what they have earned,
dismissed with peremptory words and hasty graves,
little calm tributes of the unconcerned.

Bruno, Copernicus, Shelley, Karl Marx : you
makers of victory for us : how long?
We love our lives, and the crucifixions come,
benevolent bugles smother rebellion's song,
blowing protection for the acquiescent,
and we need many strengths to continue strong.

Tendons bind us to earth, Antaeus-ridden
by desperate weakness disallied from ground,
bone of our bone; and the sky's plains above us
seduce us into powers still unfound,
and freedom's eagles scream above our faces,
misleading, sly, perverse, and unprofound.

Passage to godhead, shine illuminated
by other colors than blood and fire and pride.
Given wings, we looked downward on earth, seen
uniform from distance; and descended, tied
to the much-loved near places, moved to find
what numbers of lynched Jesuses have not been deified.

II. THE COMMITTEE–ROOM

Let us be introduced to our superiors, the voting men.
They are tired   ;   they are hungry   ;   from deciding all day
around the committee-table.
        Is it foggy outside?   It must be very foggy
        The room is white with it
The years slope into a series of nights, rocking sea-like,
shouting a black rush, enveloping time and kingdom
and the flab faces
        Those people engendered my blood swarming
        over the altar to clasp the scrolls and Menorah
        the black lips, bruised cheeks, eye-reproaches   :
        as the floor burns, singing Shema
Our little writers go about, hurrying the towns along,
running from mine to luncheon, they can't afford
to let one note escape their holy jottings:
today the mother died, festering   :   he shot himself   :   the bullet entered
the roof of the mouth, piercing the brain-pan
        How the spears went down in a flurry of blood;
        how they died howling
                how the triumph marched
        all day and all night past the beleaguered town
        blowing trumpets at the fallen towers;
        how they pulled their shoulders over the hill, crying
        for the whole regiment to hear   The Sea   The Sea
Our young men opening the eyes and mouths together,
facing the new world with their open mouths
                gibbering war
                gibbering conquest
Ha.   Will you lead us to discovery?

What did you do in school today, my darling?
        Tamburlaine rode over Genghis had a sword
        holding riot over Henry V Emperor of and

the city of Elizabeth the tall sails
crowding England into the world and Charles
his head falling many times onto a dais
how they have been monarchs and
Calvin Coolidge who wouldn't say
                              however, America

All day we have been seated around a table
                              all these many days
One day we voted on whether he was Hamlet
or whether he was himself and yesterday
I cast the deciding vote to renounce our mouths.
Today we sentinel the avenue solemnly warning
the passers (who look the other way, and cough) that we
speak with the mouths of demons, perhaps the people's,
but not our own.
                    Tomorrow
the vote's to be cast on the eyes, and sex, and brain.
Perhaps we will vote to disavow all three.
We are powerful now   :   we vote
                    death to Sacco a man's name
                    and Vanzetti a blood-brother; death
                    to Tom Mooney, or a wall, no matter;
                    poverty to Piers Plowman, shrieking anger
                    to Shelley, a cough and Fanny to Keats;
                    thus to Blake in a garden; thus to Whitman;
                    thus to D. H. Lawrence.
                              And to all you women,
                    dead and unspoken-for, what sentences,
                    to you dead children, little in the ground
              :   all you sweet generous rebels, what sentences

This is the case of one Hilliard, a native of Texas,
in the year of our Lord 1897, a freeman.
Report . . . Hilliard's power of endurance seems to be
the most wonderful thing on record.   His lower limbs
burned off a while before he became unconscious;
and his body looked to be burned to the hollow.
Was it decreed (oh coyly coyly) by an avenging God
as well as an avenging people that he suffer so?
                              We have
16 large views under magnifying glass.

8 views of the trial and the burning.
For place of exhibit watch the street bills.
                    Don't fail to see this.

Lie down dear, the day was long, the evening is smooth.
The day was long, and you were voting all day
            hammering down these heads
            tamping the mould about these diamond eyes
            filling the mouths with wax
                              lie down my dear
the bed is soft lie down to kindest dreams

            all night they carried leaves
            bore songs and garlands up the gradual hill
            the noise of singing kept the child awake
              but they were dead
            all Shakespeare's heroes   the saints   the Jews   the rebels
            but the noise stirred their graves' grass
            and the feet all falling in those places
            going up the hill with sheaves and tools
            and all the weapons of ascent together.

III. THE TRIAL

The South is green with coming spring   ;   revival
flourishes in the fields of Alabama.   Spongy with rain,
plantations breathe April   :   carwheels suck mud in the roads,
the town expands warm in the afternoons.   At night the black boy
teeters no-handed on a bicycle, whistling The St. Louis Blues,
blood beating, and hot South.   A red brick courthouse
is vicious with men inviting death.   Array your judges; call your
                                     jurors; come,
here is your justice, come out of the crazy jail.
Grass is green now in Alabama; Birmingham dusks are quiet
relaxed and soft in the park, stern at the yards:
a hundred boxcars shunted off to sidings, and the hoboes
gathering grains of sleep in forbidden corners.
In all the yards   :   Atlanta, Chattanooga,
Memphis, and New Orleans, the cars, and no jobs.

Every night the mail-planes burrow the sky,

carrying postcards to laughing girls in Texas,
passionate letters to the Charleston virgins,
words through the South   :   and no reprieve,
no pardon, no release.

A blinded statue attends before the courthouse,
bronze and black men lie on the grass, waiting,
the khaki dapper National Guard leans on its bayonets.
But the air is populous beyond our vision:
all the people's anger finds its vortex here
as the mythic lips of justice open, and speak.

Hammers and sickles are carried in a wave of strength, fire-tipped,
swinging passionately ninefold to a shore.
Answer the back-thrown Negro face of the lynched, the flat forehead
                                        knotted,
the eyes showing a wild iris, the mouth a welter of blood,
answer the broken shoulders and these twisted arms.
John Brown, Nat Turner, Toussaint stand in this courtroom,
Dred Scott wrestles for freedom there in the dark corner,
all our celebrated shambles are repeated here   :   now again
Sacco and Vanzetti walk to a chair, to the straps and rivets
and the switch spitting death and Massachusetts' will.
Wreaths are brought out of history
    here are the well-nourished flowers of France, grown strong on blood,
    Caesar twisting his thin throat toward conquest, turning north from
                            the Roman laurels,
    the Istrian galleys slide again to sea.
    How they waded through bloody Godfrey's Jerusalem   !
    How the fires broke through Europe, and the rich
    and the tall jails battened on revolution   !
    The fastidious Louis', cousins to the sun, stamping
    those ribboned heels on Calas, on the people;
    the lynched five thousand of America.
    Tom Mooney from San Quentin, Herndon   :   here
    is an army for audience
                        all resolved
to a gobbet of tobacco, spat, and the empanelled hundred,
a jury of vengeance, the cheap pressed lips, the narrow eyes like
                            hardware;
the judge, his eye-sockets and cheeks dark and immutably secret,
the twisting mouth of the prosecuting attorney.

Nine dark boys spread their breasts against Alabama,
schooled in the cells, fathered by want.
   Mother : one writes : they treat us bad.   If they send us
   back to Kilby jail, I think I shall kill myself.
   I think I must hang myself by my overalls.

Alabama and the South are soft with spring;
in the North, the seasons change, sweet April, December and the air
loaded with snow.   There is time for meetings
during the years, they remaining in prison.
                            In the Square
a crowd listens, carrying banners.
Overhead, boring through the speaker's voice, a plane
circles with a snoring of motors revolving in the sky,
drowning the single voice.   It does not touch
the crowd's silence.   It circles.   The name stands :
Scottsboro

       .   .   .   .   .

Earth, include sky ; air, be stable to our
feet, which have need of stone and iron stance;
all opposites, affirm your contradictions,
lead, all you prophets, our mechanic dance.

Arches over the earth, conform, be still,
calm Roman in the evening cool of grace,
dramatic Gothic, be finally rounded now
pared equal to the clean savannahs of space,

grind levels to one plane, unfold the stones
that shaped you pointed, return to ground, return,
bird be no more a brand upon the sky
no more a torch to which earth's bodies burn

fire attracting fire in magnetism
too subtle for dissection and proponence,
torturing fire, crucifying posture
with which dead Jesus quenches his opponents.

Shall we then straddle Jesus in a plane
the rigid crucified revived at last
the pale lips flattened in a wind a rain

of merging conquered blast and counterblast.
Shout to us   :   See   !
the wind   !
Shout to us   :
FLY

THE TUNNEL

I.

NO WORK is master of the mine today
tyrant that walks with the feet of murder here
under his cracked shoes a grass-blade dusted
dingy with coal's smear.

The father's hand is rubbed with dust, his body
is witness to coal, black glosses all his skin.
Around the pithead they stand and do not talk
looking at the obvious sign.

Behind his shoulder stands the black mountain
of unbought coal, green-topped with grass growing
rank in the shag, as if coal were native earth
and the top a green snowing

down on the countryside.   In the whole valley
eleven mines, and five of them are closed,
two are on strike, but in the others, workers
scramble down the shafts, disposed

to grub all day and all night, lording it
in the town because of their jobs and their bosses
at work with all the other mines graveyards.
These are the valley's losses

which even the company fails to itemize
in stubborn black and red in the company stores   :
the empty breasts like rinds, the father's hands,
the sign, the infected whores,

a puppy roasted for pregnant Mary's dinner . . .
On the cold evenings the jobless miners meet
wandering dully attracted to the poolroom,
walking down the grey street.

"Well," says the father, "nothing comes of this,
the strippings run to weeds, the roads all mucked.
A dead mine makes dead miners.   God, but I
was a fool not to have chucked

the whole damned ruin when I was a kid."
"And how'd you have a chance to throw it over?"
"Well," he said, "if I hadn't married   :   though then
the place had more in its favor.

Babies came quickly after summertimes.
You could work, and quit, and get a better job.
God knows if it'll ever be the same,
or if ever they'll think not to rob,

not to cut wages, not to weigh us short."
"All right," the other says, "maybe God does.
We'll be a long time dead, come that time, buried
under coal where our life was;

we were children and did not know our childhood,
we got infants, and never knew our wives,
year in and out, seeing no color but coal,
we were the living who could not have their lives."

II.

Emerge, city, from your evening   :   allay me, sleep   :
but the city withdraws to night, sleep passes whitely
inanely over my eyelids mockcomforting pale dawn's
developing silver and I unloved.

Shall we no more, my love, pass down the lanes of grace
slowly together and in each other's safekeeping, no more
shall I watch evening touch hands to your face
and feel myself glisten in answer?

Day shines a last gloom quickening the street, and deep
grave-deep the subway files down space to a moment
over me a plane exterminates distance   ;   you
are unalterably removed   :   day touches you

nor night though tiger it may rage abroad   ;   you are
beyond its claws, if my love will not reach you.
O love, how am I surpassed how mocked   how
defiled and corroded untouched by your kiss.

I came to you riding on love with love in my hands, advancing
seaworn, hearing far bells   :   you have been a prow
carving a tragic sea to meet my love, you have been lamps
burning all night over tired waters.

You have been stone set upon fine-grained woods, buildings
of granite standing in a street of stone, roads
full of fallen flowers wet under the foot, ships
pointing an index to voyage among islands,

blue archipelagoes   :   your body being an island
set about with magnetic flowers and flesh and fruit   :
the sons I might bear you, the sons, the fragrant daughters.
Intrudes on this the bleak authentic voice   :

wherefore does the mouth stiffen, the cheeks freeze austere
as stone, affording special grief among the days
and cold days catalogued of comfort murdered,
the iron passage, estranged eyes, and the death

of all my logic   :   pale with the weakness of one
dead and not yet arisen, a hollow bath of flame
with my fire low along the oils of grace
how many deaths, body so torn from spirit.

Body, return   :   I love you   :   soul, come home!
I am gone down to death in a great bleeding.
All day the bleeding washes down my sides   ;   at night
darkly and helplessly my face is wet.

Open me a refuge where I may be renewed.   Speak to me
world hissing over cables, shining among steel strands,
plucking speech out on a wire, linking voices,
reach me now in my fierceness, or I am drowned

buried among my flesh, dead of a dead desire.
All night I went to the places of my love,
opened to one wished meeting, all unarmed.
And there was nothing but machine-loud streets.

All night I returned to the places of my love.
My love escaped me.   May not the blood's frail drums
ever pulse healing in wrists and lips made known
whispering convalescence through a mist of sleep?

Let me approach infinity in love and sorrow, waiting
with the doubled strength of my own will and love,
burning with copper-spun electric fire, unconsumed,
a bush upon a barren darkening plain.

My blood must be fed on foreign substance, lacking
the knowledge of those gestures, roots of words, unfeeling
the wet intestinal movings of another body, starving
not knowing the muscles' flexing.

Shall we losing our ego gain it, saddening
after no response and a turning away?   Sheer
the skyscrapers stand, pure without meaning, single
in desire rising to touch the sky   :

the diver waits, arms thrust in white dihedral
to air and next moment's water   :   the flash of shock
travels through diver   lover   tower   plane   reaching
sky, a contact in desire, leaving

bondage in flight.   Sever the cords binding our bones,
loosen us to each other, approach, night, return me love   :
unblind me, give me back myself, touch me now   :
slide, night, into the climates of the mind.

III.

The cattle-trains edge along the river, bringing morning on a white vibration
breaking the darkness split with beast-cries   :   a milk-wagon proceeds
down the street leaving the cold bottles   :   the Mack truck pushes
around the corner, tires hissing on the washed asphalt.   A clear sky
growing candid and later bright.
                              Ceiling unlimited.   Visibility unlimited.

2 They stir on the pillows, her leg moving, her face swung windowward
vacant with sleep still, modeled with light's coming   ;   his dark head
among the softness of her arm and breast, nuzzled in dreams,
mumbling the old words, hardly roused.   They return to silence.
                    At the airport, the floodlights are snapped off.

3 Turning, he says; "Tell me how's the sky this morning?" "Fair," she answers,
"no clouds from where I lie; bluer and bluer."   "And later and later—
god, for some sleep into some noon, instead of all these mornings
with my mouth going stiff behind the cowling and wind brushing
away from me and my teeth freezing against the wind."
                    Light gales from the northwest   :   tomorrow, rain.

4 The street is long, with a sprinkling of ashcans   ;   panhandlers
begin to forage among banana-peels and cardboard boxes.
She moves to the window, tall and dark before a brightening sky,
full with her six-months' pregnancy molded in ripeness.
                    Stands, watching the sky's blankness.

5 Very soon   :   "How I love to see you when I wake," he says,
"How the child's meaning in you is my life's growing."
She faces him, hands brought to her belly's level, offering,
wordless, looking upon him.   She carries his desire well.
                    Sun rises   :   6:38 A.M.   Sun sets. . . .

6 "Flying is what makes you strange to me, dark as Asia,
almost removed from my world even in your closenesses   :
that you should be familiar with those intricacies
and a hero in mysteries which all the world has wanted."
                    Wind velocity changing from 19 to 30.

7 "No, that's wrong," and he laughs, "no personal hero's left
to make a legend.   Those centuries have gone.   If I fly,
why, I know that countries are not map-colored, that seas
belong to no one, that war's a pock-marking on Europe   :   "
                    The Weather Bureau's forecast, effective until noon.

8 "Your friends sleep with strange women desperately,
drink liquor and sleep heavily to forget those skies.
You fly all day and come home truly returning
to me who know only land.   And we will have this child."
                    New York to Boston   :   Scattered to broken clouds.

9 "The child will have a hard time to be an American,"
he says slowly, "fathered by a man whose country is air,
who believes there are no heroes to withstand
wind, or a loose bolt, or a tank empty of gas."
                    To Washington   :   Broken clouds becoming overcast.

10 "It will be a brave child," she answers, smiling.
"We will show planes to it, and the bums in the street.
You will teach it to fly, and I will love it
very much."   He thinks of his job, dressing.
                    Strong west northwest winds above 1000 feet.

11 He thinks how many men have wanted flight.
He ties his tie, looking into his face.·
Finishes breakfast, hurrying to be gone,
crossing the river to the airport and his place.
                    To Cleveland   :   Broken clouds to overcast.

12 She does not imagine how the propeller turns
in a blinding speed, swinging the plane through space;
she never sees the cowling rattle and slip
forward and forward against the grim blades' grinding.
                    Cruising speed 1700 R.P.M.

13 Slipping, a failing desire   ;   slipping like death
insidious against the propeller, until the blades shake,
bitten by steel, jagged against steel, broken,
and his face angry and raked by death, staring.
                    Strong west northwest or west winds above 2000 feet.

14 She watches the clock as his return time hurries,
the schedule ticking off, eating the short minutes.
She watches evening advance   ;   she knows the child's stirring.
She knows night.   She knows he will not come.
                    Ceiling unlimited.   Visibility unlimited.

.   .   .   .   .

The rough skin dusty with coal on the slack·hands   ;
lover trailing regret through the evening streets
uncomforted, walking toward destruction   :
the mouth of the young pilot stiffening

(I love to see you when I wake at morning)
hurtling, spiralling that plucks the breath from the throat
in a long chute to gauged mechanic death.

Greyly our vigor seeps away, the fingers
weak and the lips unspeaking, somberly
devoid of wholeness are we drowned again
mumbling death as our cheeks stiffen
as we go down these maelstroms   :   dissolution.
   Harsh blue screams summer from behind the plane
   the sea stiffens under it sculpturally.
   Split space, monotonous and even-winged,
   continue toward despair methodically.
Destruction and a burning fill these lives
unloved incompetent they compromise
with death and the bases of emotion fearing
the natural calm inclusiveness of time.
   Tigers follow in a splendor of motion
   sleek death treads unperturbed among these things,
   time rages like a tiger and the
   savage defeat swallows the fallen wings
plunging
O Icarus accurate white into the sea
the wax support too trusted   ;   the white pride
in sovereignty collapsed   ;   go down to harbor,
go down, plane, to the water's eagerness
engulfed, plunging

     .   .   .   .   .

We have prayed torrents of humility, open
in anguish to be hurt, in terror to be fooled.
We are beyond demand, waiting a minute
unconscious in attendance   :   here is strength to be used
delicately, most subtly on the controls and levers.
They begged that time be condensed.   Extend space for us,
let us include this memory in ourselves,
time and our dividend of history.

THE STRUCTURE OF THE PLANE

I. THE STRUCTURE OF THE PLANE

Kitty Hawk is a Caesar among monuments   ;
the stiff bland soldiers predestined to their death
the bombs piled neatly like children's marbles piled
sperm to breed corpses eugenically by youth
out of seductive death.
The hill outdoes our towers
we might treasure a thistle grown from a cannon-mouth
they have not permitted rust and scum and blossoms
to dirty the steel,
however we have the plane
the hill, flower among monuments.

"To work intelligently" (Orville and Wilbur Wright)
"one needs to know the effects of variations
incorporated in the surfaces. . . . The pressures on squares
are different from those on rectangles, circles, triangles, or ellipses . . .
The shape of the edge also makes a difference."

The plane is wheeled out of the hangar.   The sleeves shake
fixing the wind, the four o'clock blue sky
blinks in the goggles swinging over his wrist.
The plane rests, the mechanic in cream-colored overalls
encourages the engine into idling speed.
The instructor looks at his class
and begins the demonstration.

"We finally became discouraged, and returned to kite-flying.
But as we grew older we had to give up this sport,
it was unbecoming to boys of our ages."

On the first stroke of the piston the intake valve opens,
the piston moves slowly from the head of the cylinder,

drawing in its mixture of gas and air.   On the second stroke
the piston returns, the valve closes.   The mixture is compressed.
A spark occurs, igniting America, opening India,
finding the Northwest Passage, Cipango spice,
causing the mixture to burn, expanding the gases
which push the piston away on the power stroke.
The final exhaust stroke serves to release the gases,
allowing the piston to scavenge the cylinder.
                We burn space, we sever galaxies,
                solar systems whirl about Shelley's head,
                we give ourselves ease, gentlemen, art and these explosions
                and Peter Ronsard finger-deep in roses   ;
gentlemen, remember these incandescent points,
remember to check, remember to drain the oil,
remember Plato O remember me
                the college pathways rise
                the president's voice intoning sonnets
                the impress of hoofmarks on the bridle path
                the shining girls the lost virginities
                the plane over a skeletal water-tower
                our youth dissolving O remember
                romantically dissolving remember me.

Blue smoke from the exhaust signifies too much oil.
Save yourselves from excesses, dirt, and tailspins.
These are the axioms   :   stability, control,
and equilibrium   :   in a yaw, in a roll, or pitch.
Here, gentlemen, are the wings, of fabric doped and painted
here is the rudder
here the propeller spins
:   BE   hammers in the brain
FLY and the footbeat of that drum
may not be contradicted
must be mine
must be made ours, say the brothers Wright together
                although the general public had been invited
                few dared a cold December
                in order to see another plane not fly.

The helmet is strapped tight, orders are shouted
the elbows of steel move in oil
air is forced under the ship, the pilot's hand

is safe on the stick, the young student sits
with the wind mottling his eyelashes, rigidly.
Centuries fall behind his brain, the motor
pushes in a four-beat rhythm, his blood moves,
he dares look at the levels mounting in clouds
the dropping fields of the sky the diminishment of earth   ;
                now he thinks I am the child crying Mother
                this rim is the threshold into the hall's night
                or the windowsill livened with narcissus.
                The white edge of the bath a moment before
                slipping into watery ease, the windowsill
                eager for the jump into the street
                the hard stone under my back, the earth
                with its eyes and hands its eyes and hands
                its eyes
                        fixed eyes on the diminishing
                take me back the bath had fronds of steam
                escaping the hands held my head
                my eyes slipped in oil looking along your beauty
                earth is painful the distance hurts
                mother the night, the distance, dear
he is standing with one look of hate upon him
screams at the pilot you bastard, you bastard, jumps
trailing a long scream above him, the plane yaws down,
the motor pulls heavily, the ground is dark November,
his parachute opens a bright plume surrendering downward,
the plane heads up again, no good in following,
continues unfascinated by night or land or death.

II. THE STRIKE

"Well," he said, "George, I never thought you were with us.
You walked out of the shaft as if you'd spent years of your life
planning some day to walk out once without blinking
and not stop for a smoke but walk over to our side."

"No," he said, "I never expected to.   It was only the last cut:
before that, I'd have worked no matter who starved first."
The snow was stamped down with black nailprints
the stamping was a drum to warm them, stiff veins, crusted hands.

"Carrying guns, boys!" said the director.   "Now, boys;
I'll speak to the others and see what I can do."
The heavy-set miner spat on the peel of snow.
The fingers weighed on the triggers.   December bit
into the bone, into the tight skulls, creaking one word.

Tell how the men watched the table, a plate of light,
the rigid faces lit around it, the mouths
opening and clamping, the little warmth
watched against the shafts of the breakers.
Tell how the men watched.
Tell how the child chewed its shoe to strips.

That day broke equal grey, the lockers empty,
the cages hanging in a depth of silence.
Shall we say   :   there were two lines at last   :
death played like a current between them, playing,
the little flames of death ran along those eyes   :   ?

Death faced the men with a desperate seduction,
lifted a hand with the skill of a hypnotist.
They were so ready in khaki with bayonets.
          "George!" he heard.   That had once been his name.
          Very carefully he had stepped from his place,
          walked over his ground, over the last line.
          It seemed impossible he should not die.
                    When a gun faces you, look down the bore,
                    that is the well of death   :   when it confronts you
                    it is not satisfied, it draws you steadily
                    more loving than love, eagerer than hunger,
                    resolving all unbalance.   He went to it.

However, the line held.   The plump men raised themselves
up from the chairs in a dreary passion of wrath,
hoisted themselves to the doorway.   Spoke.
There was his body, purpled, death casing him
in ice and velvet and sleep.   Indeed, they spoke,
this was unwarranted.   No, they conceded.   No.
Perhaps the strike might equal victory,
a company funeral, and the trucks of coal
                    ladled up from the earth,
                    heaped on this grave.

III. THE LOVER

Answer with me these certainties
of glands swelling with sentiment
the loves embittered the salts and waters mixing
a chemic threatening destruction.

Answer the men walking toward death
leaping to death meeting death in a kiss
able to find of equilibrium none
except that last of hard stone kissing stone.

Answer the lover's questioning in the streets
the evenings domed with purple, the bones
easing, the flesh slipping perfume upon the air   :
all surfaces of flight are pared to planes

equal, equilibrated, solid in fulfilment.   No way
is wanted to escape, no explosions craved,
only this desire must be met, this motion
be balanced with passion   ;

     in the wreaths of time given to us what love
     may reach us in the streets . the books   the years
     what wreaths of love may touch our dreams,
     what skeins of fine response may clothe our flesh,
     robe us in valor brave as our dear wish

     lover haunting the ghosts of rivers, letting time
     slide a fluid runner into darkness
     give over the sad eyes the marble face of pain
     do not mourn   :   remember   :   do not forget
     but never let this treason play you mate,

     take to yourself the branches of green trees
     watch the clean sky signed by the flight of planes
     know rivers of love   be flooded thoroughly
     by love and the years and the past and know
     the green tree perishes and green trees grow.

Knock at the doors   ;   go to the windows   ;   run,
you will not find her soon who, lost in love,

relinquished last month to that silver music
repeating in her throat forsaken tunes.

Rigid and poised for the latest of these lovers
she stretches acute in waiting on the bed
most avaricious for the length of arms
the subtle thighs and heavy confident head.

Taut with a steel strut's singing tautness she
clinches her softness anguished at postponement
hardening all her thought she swears to be
unpacified by minutes of atonement.

The ticking of an ormolu clock taxes
her body with time's weight.   The opened door
adjusts such things   ;   responsive, she relaxes
ringing in answer to a word before

all tensity is changed to eagerness.
Translated and resolved, the anguish through,
sensitive altogether to the present   :
"Now?"   "Yes," she says, "yes," she says, "do."

                .   .   .   .   .

Answer motion with motion, be birds flying
be the enormous movements of the snows,
be rain, be love, remain equilibrated
unseeking death,
                    if you must have pilgrimages
go travelling to balance need with answer
suiting the explosion to the ensuing shock
the foil to the airstream running over it
food to the mouth, tools to the body, mind
to the bright mind that leaps in necessity
go answering   answering   FLY

NIGHT FLIGHT : NEW YORK

Lucid at dusk the city lies revealed
authentic purpose under masonry
emerging into emphasis.   Tenuous
the bodies grim at noon lie scattered, limp
on the beach of evening, and the long sea
of night softly encroaches on reality.

Pale the primitive blue of afternoon,
morning's bravado made ambiguous,
and all the bulwarks we relied upon
relapsed to fluid concept.   Now the night
opens a shady empire odorous
prodigal in sweetness, sweetly promiscuous.

Foliate evening opens in a blur
of even color on the risen stone   :
in unified unbroken shoulderings
of tower past planned tower, twilight-softened;
insanest noise resolves to monotone.
The theory of the city's fact made known

in a revelatory evening stillness.
Traffic and work and riot, triad of waking
are garbled into a full chord, drowning
identity in conquering vibration
impinging on the air, loud, rising, making
the city conscious of propellers shaking

hard frames of aircraft   ;   night cloven by twin wings,
incisive angles ripping evening where
blueness was closing deepest to the north
beyond the Bridge, beyond the island, planes   :
a burr of dissonance, a swoop of bare
fatal battalions black against the air.

Time is metric now with the regular advance   :   descend the skytrack
signal-red on the wingtips, defined by a glitter of bulbs   ;

we lean at the windows or roofrails, attentive
under inverted amphitheatre of sky.
The river is keen under blackness, weapon-malevolent,
crossed jagged marks mirrored against its steel.
Suddenly from a trance of speed are let fall bubbles slowly
blooming in pale light, but hardening to crystal
glows, into calcium brilliance, white bombs floating imperturbable
along the planes of the air, in chains of burning, destruction in the wake
of the beautiful transition.   City, shimmer in amusement,
spectators at the mocking of your bombardment.
City, cry out   :   the space is full of planes, you will be heard,
            the thin shark-bodies are concentrated to listen,
without a sound but the clean strength of the engines, dripping death-globes
            drifting down the wind
lifted by parachutes in a metaphor of death,
the symbol not the substance, merest detail of fact, going down
the wincing illuminated river, fading over the city.
Planes weave   :   the children laugh at the fireworks   :   "Oh, pretty stars!
                                        Oh, see the white!"

Planes move in a calculated dance of war
each throwing, climax to superbest flight.

No whisper rises from the city   :   New York is quiet
as a doped man walking to the electric chair, fixed in memory,
suspended in an image of peace.   Skeins of light
are woven above the city, gathering-in evening in a harvest of peace,
from loveliest vessels falling, the buds of annihilation.
Turn and re-turn in precise advance, engines of power
subtle terrific potency, rays of destruction emitted from black suns
shining the faces of burial, loosing magnificence
in bombs, in a sardonic joke play games of death,
cancel the city to an achievement   :   zero.

Pregnant zero breeding annihilation. . . .
Futility stands clear on these horizons
marked in the zeros of a thousand clouds
pregnant above a harvested land, whose fruit
was peace infected with the germs of war.
In tragic streaks the planes' formations fly
across the black pavilions of the sky.

         .   .   .   .   .

Failure encompassed in success, the warplanes
dropping flares, as a historic sum of knowledge,
tallying Icarus loving the sun, and plunging,
Leonardo engraved on the Florentine pale evening
scheming toward wings, as toward an alchemy
transferring life to golden circumstance.
Following him, the warplanes travelling home,
flying over the cities, over the minds
of cities rising against imminent doom.
Icarus' passion, Da Vinci's skill, corrupt,
all rotted into war   :

Between murmur and murmur, birth and death,
is the earth's turning which follows the earth's turning,
a swift whisper of life, an ambiguous word spoken   ;
morning travelling quiet on mutinous fields,
muscles swollen tight in giant effort   ;   rain   ;   some stars   ;
a propeller's glimpsing silver whirl, intensely upward,
intensely forward, bearing the plane   :   flying.

Believe that we bloom upon this stalk of time   ;
and in this expansion, time too grows for us
richer and richer towards infinity.
They promised us the gold and harps and seraphs.
Our rising and going to sleep is better than future pinions.
We surrender that hope, drawing our own days in,
covering space and time draped in tornadoes,
lightning invention, speed crushing the stars upon us,
stretching the accordion of our lives, sounding the same chord
longer and savoring it until the echo fails.
Believe that your presences are strong,
O be convinced without formula or rhyme
or any dogma   ;   use yourselves   :   be   :   fly.
Believe that we bloom upon this stalk of time.

T H E O R Y   O F   F L I G H T

You dynamiting the structure of our loves
embrace your lovers solving antithesis,
open your flesh, people, to opposites
conclude the bold configuration, finish
the counterpoint   :   sky, include earth now.
Flying, a long vole of descent
renders us land again.
Flight is intolerable contradiction.
We bear the bursting seeds of our return
we will not retreat   ;   never be moved.
Stretch us onward   include in us the past
sow in us history, make us remember triumph.
   O golden fructifying, O the sonorous calls
   to arms and embattled mottoes in one war
   brain versus brain for absolutes, ring harsh!
   Miners rest from blackness   :   reapers, lay by the sheaves
   forgive us our tears   we go to victory
   in a commune of regenerated lives.
   The birds of flight return, crucified shapes
   old deaths restoring vigor through the sky
   mergent with earth, no more horizons now
   no more unvisioned capes, no death   ;   we fly.

      .   .   .   .   .

Answer together the birds' flying
reconcile rest to rest
motion to motion's poise,
     the guns are dying the past is born again
     into these future minds the incarnate past
     gleaming upon the present
                    fliers, grave men,
    lovers   :   do not stop to remember these,
    think of them as you travel, the tall kind prophets,
    the flamboyant leapers toward death,
    the little painful children
                  how the veins were slit

into the Roman basins to fill Europe with blood
how our world has run over bloody with love and blood
and the misuses of love and blood and veins.
Now we arrive to meet ourselves at last,
we cry beginnings
the criers in the midnight streets call dawn   ;
respond   respond
you workers   poets   men of science and love.

Now we can look at our subtle jointures, study our hands,
the tools are assembled, the maps unrolled, propellers spun,
do we say **all is in readiness   :**
the times approach, here is the signal shock   :   ?

Master in the plane shouts "Contact"   :
master on the ground   :   "Contact!"
    he looks up   :   "Now?" whispering   :   "Now."
    "Yes," she says.   "Do."
    Say yes, people.
    Say yes.
    YES

THE BLOOD IS JUSTIFIED

FOR MEMORY

For Ruth Lehman
obit February 10, 1934

I. LIFE AND WORKS

Open with care the journal of those years
firm years precipitating days to death
This was my friend walking in color and flame
walking through a texture of sense
                            no breath
deranges her fine hair   no voice changes her face.

It is hardly possible she will not come again
returned for a short while out of distances
to be re-given to distance and her loves.
It is hardly truth to say that soon
a letter will not come, postmarked Detroit,
New Orleans, Chicago, ultimate Mexico.
I think she must come, and go, and come again.

Throatfuls of life, arms crammed with brilliant days,
the colored years beat strength upon her youth,
pain-bombs exploded her body, joy rocketed in her,
the stranger forests, the books, the bitter times,
preluded college in a sheltered town.
        Remember the pale suede jacket and russet coat
        swinging down avenues of trees together,
        the nights of talk   light cast from copper bowls,
        the fugitive journey to the coal-hills   :   names,
        Del Thomas, Tony Mancuso, Mrs. Silva,
        the black river curdling under a midnight wind.
        Remember how the pale wrists flickered love,
        the dark eye-sockets impelled her to the poor,
          ring changes
          tell of the loves in her life
          tell how she loved.

This was my friend of whom I knew the face
the steel-straight intellect, broidered fantastic dreams
the quarrel by the lake
and knew the hopes

              She died.   And must be dead.
And is not dead where memory prevails.

Cut the stone, deepen her name.
Her mother did not know her.
Her friends were not enough, we missed essentials.
Love was enough and its blossoms.   Behind her life
stands a tall flower-tree, around her life
are worked her valid words into her testament
of love and writing and a ring of love.

II. HOLY DYING

Across the country, iron hands push up chimneys
black fingers stuck up from the blackened ground.
The rivers bend seaward urgent in blue reaches;
her pain turned seaward.   Her life extended past
the sea, the cities, the individual poor,
passionate and companioned, following life.

        Through the bright years reckless and proud
        dimming into that last impossible pain.
        We cannot think she will not come again.
        The words lean on the written line, the page
        is a signal fire   all the letters shine.
        Into this life is lowered now death's sign,
        the young days flicker up, the poems burn,
        we cannot say Return.

Slowly her death is propelled into our lives
the yellow message   the clipped convenient style
the cancelled stamps   the telephone wires ring
confirming fear "You were right"   :   in a week's short while.
Her love was never handcuffed, her hates spoke up,
her life was a job of freedom.
              Now the news comes, the **Times** prints a name
             the telephone rings short music over her.

Drink your coffee, open your throat for words.
Loving, she died in passion and holiness.
They share remorse who had required less.

III. RITUAL FOR DEATH

Last night she died
Turn down the lamps tonight
shade the walls
                    let the proud voices rise
out of the midnight street,   the whistle flying
up and along and flying in the street
the harsh struck stone,   a brake squealing the pause
and the brave silence after a lapse of sound.

Turn out the lights
Her body does not move
is striding over no hill in all the world
there is no avenue in Illinois shall know
the eager mouth,   the fine voluptuous hands
touch no more Mexicos in dream again.
There was a shadow deep along her cheek,
her eyes and hair were intricate with sun.
Now lights are out.
:   Stand to me in the dark
Set your mouth on me for friends we did not know
Be strong in love
give strength to all we meet
the loving   the kind   the proletarian strong
convey our love to her in the grey fields
less grey for her, send her our breathing lives.
This was my friend
                    forget the "my," speak out
This was my friend who   eager   rash   and brave
has found one answer in an early grave.
This is my body   :   in its youth I find
strength given from the startle of her mind.
If we have strength in this evening, force life between her lips
        seal it   convey it   post it   the sheet discolored
        the ink already fading
                        the dead words fading
                        the dead all dead.

Out of the South are vivid flowers sent,
African daisies, red anemone   :
here are the riches of a continent,
and intellectual gifts   breaking you free,
poetry sounding in the narrow skull
sealing the sutures with music,   smoothing the cheek
with vocable comfort   the long hands of sorrow.
The full-blown flowers are given   :   our hands are full
of flowers and gestures   :   across New England dunes
where the stiff grasses rise against the sea,
across the city   the dark-red roofs, the stone,
across the Alleghanies,   down the Valley
the air speaks plenty   the words have all been spoken.

   Upon what skies are these ambitions written?
   across what field lies scattered the young wish,
   beneath what seas toll all those fallen dreams——?

CITY OF MONUMENTS

Washington 1934

Be proud   you people   of these graves
    these chiseled words   this precedent
From these blind ruins shines our monument.

Dead navies of the brain will sail
    stone celebrate its final choice
    when the air shakes, a single voice
a strong voice able to prevail   :

Entrust no hope to stone although the stone
shelter the root   :   see too-great burdens placed
with nothing certain but the risk
set on the infirm column of
the high memorial obelisk

erect in accusation sprung against
a barren sky taut over Anacostia   :
give over, Gettysburg   !   a word will shake your glory   :
blood of the starved fell thin upon this plain,
this battle is not buried with its slain.

    Gravestone and battlefield retire
    the whole green South is shadowed dark,
    the slick white domes are cast in night.
    But uneclipsed above the park

    the veteran of the Civil War
    sees havoc in the tended graves
    the midnight bugles blown to free
    still unemancipated slaves.

Blinded by chromium or transfiguration
we watch, as through a microscope, decay   :
    down the broad streets the limousines
advance in passions of display.

Air glints with diamonds, and these clavicles
emerge through orchids by whose trailing spoor
the sensitive cannot mistake
the implicit anguish of the poor.

The throats incline, the marble men rejoice
careless of torrents of despair.

Split by a tendril of revolt
stone cedes to blossom everywhere.

STUDY IN A LATE SUBWAY

The moon revolves outside; possibly, black air
turns so around them facing night's concave,
momentum the slogan of their hurling brains
swung into speed, crying for stillness   high
        suspended and rising on time's wave.

Did these tracks have a wilder life in the ground?
beaten from streams of metal in secret earth   :
energy travels along the veins of steel,
their faces rush forward, missiles of discontent
        thrown vaguely to the south and north.

That head is jointed loosely on his neck,
his glossy eyes turn on the walls and floor   :
her face is a blank breast with sorrow
spouting at the mouth's nipple.   All eyes move
        heavily to the opening door,

regarding in dullness how we also enter.
An angle of track charges up to us, swings
out and past in a firework of signals.
Sleepily others dangle by one hand
        tense and semi-crucified things.

Speed welcomes us in explosions of night   :   here
is wrath and fortitude and motion's burning   :
the world buries the directionless, until
the heads are sprung in awareness or drowned in peace.
        Sleep will happen.   We must give them morning.

CHILD AND MOTHER

for Vega Hustana

Revolution shall be a toy of peace to you,
children during our effort.   Storm covers all our days
the tracts of sunlight overcome with thunder
black on this ocean and our youth going.
Slowly our world is shaped to a new country
for living minute fingers, the duplicated flesh   :
The old will surrender, forced under; they endure
though dead adults walk stiffly in the street
cramming the dead poor in their mouths for meat.

Seashores of centuries
all cosmic whisperings
ripple upon this beach,
listen until she sings
lullaby to all sudden
all grievous things.

Rome fashioned you blankets
Asia, a coverlet,
we live for your smiling   :
sleep, we shall not forget   ;
these worlds are straining
to make your Soviet.

Beaches of darkness! the transparent foam-lips hurrying, pouring
spent on the margin trailing sea-currents
mid-ocean streams   :   at the sand, ankle-deep
mother with child braced in the hip's firm socket
fronting the torrents.

Nakedly to the extreme of the world come bathers
advancing, the pale skin pathetic against the sea,
untried and bare   :   the flesh, the bones' thin tubes
facing dim oceans, raving hurricane, windspill,
leviathan-tyranny.

Child, you shall grow to follow,
survive, and find
wet hollow, submarine terror
not so unkind
as to blast strength, your eyes
unsealed, and an armed mind.

Child leans the dark head against protective side
turning its look softly to the horizon
moving its hand along the rapid wind.
The mother knows this ocean and will tell
clews to the young eyes' candor, fertile thoughts
will be asserted.
                  Rage, ocean   :   foam, oppressions,
We stand, and these children follow, and all will yet be well.

Chaos is split   :   the first slow definite strides
are taken against the open waters   ;   be
fresh growth, be confident for braveries
   we and our children meet these tides
prows of revolt launched among barbarous seas.

ECCENTRIC MOTION

Dashing in glass we race,
New York to Washington   :
encased with bubbles lie
in emerald spa   :
upholstered promenades
convey us far.
Have we reached the last limits?
What have we not done?

Shut into velvet we
survey the scene,
the locked-up building,
the frozen pier   :
before and before the events,
we loved our minds in fear   :
they wriggle into worms.
We watch.   We turn.   Surrounded,
we are at last closed in.

Coated in learning, do we
cause its crown to fall?
the plane, the bath, the car
extend our protection   :
(But have we seen it all?
Shall we continue
in this direction?   :   )

This is not the way   •
to save the day.
Get up and dress and go
nobly to and fro   :
Dashing in glass we race,
New York to Mexico. . . .

SUNDAYS, THEY SLEEP LATE

The days are incestuous, each with its yesterday,
and they, walking heavily in the streets, atone for the moment's
sin :   their memories laboring under the weight of today
in its perverse alliance with the past.   Laments

are heard, droning from the city on all other mornings
but Sundays, they sleep late, and need not cry to wake,
sniffling in the pillow, realizing the day's churnings
of minute resolving to minute, and the whole day slack,

the wind bled of vigor, the talk in the parlor
of people pasturing on each other's minds, and sunset
evolving in the air, a quiet change against the duller
signs in pandemonium of day's gradual transit:

the klaxon voices through the roads, the picnickers joking
(returning from the fields), who wept before they dressed.
On Sundays their dreams are longer, and their waking
is a long exhalation of their weeks, decompressed.

There are these things to be remembered: the nine boys waiting,
battle-fronts of the rising army with holes bitten by death,
the man in the prison overland, and history beating
out the recurrent facts of power, suppression, wrath.

The days are incestuous.   They witness the daily binding
of minutes linking backwards.   Their remembering atones
in no part for the things they remember.   They sink in blinding
sleep too long, they dissolve in sleep their remembering bones.

THOUSANDS OF DAYS

Morning cried by the bed　:
at Seven, I understood　—
by Eight, I was very God,
happiness in my head.

At Nine, I went to work,
and all the machines spoke　:
Quiet there!　　Don't talk,
make, break and make　!

At Ten, I opened my book
and all that hour I read
'The tallest men are dead,
their graveyard's in your look. . . .'

I rose, angered, through sky
in a plane of glass,
dreaming speed, I pass
very bright, very high.

As it went up toward Noon
I heard the sun scream　:
fly, suck your yellow dream,
we'll end it soon.

I fell all through One,
howling and threatening,
until at Two I sing
of a far reunion　:

On Three the masses spread,
a fist opening bare,
a great hand in the square
to vindicate the dead.

By Four the men had gone,
the land was wet with rain

and a fountain stood up plain
on every lawn.

The clock picked at Five,
those jets turned silver then
with the lovely words of men
who wrote and remained alive,

prophesying the night
of Six, and the dawn behind   ;
but, creeping down the wind,
Seven snatched all the light.

Now am I left alone
waiting for day   :
sometimes I turn away,
sometimes I sleep like stone.

Midnight is on my heels,
death bites about my legs.
While all my courage sags
the endless night wheels,

danger yells, and with
this blackness comes
back confidence, and blooms
in song and act and myth.

Call off your black dog, death,
it cannot bark me down   :
I'll travel past these wounds
and speak another breath   !

THE SURROUNDED

They escape before, but their shadows walk behind,
filling the city with formidable dark,
spilling black over the sun's run gold, speeding a rumor
of warfare and the sciences of death, and work
of treason and exposure, following
me for an easy mark.

The sky is travelled by brightness, clouds ignite,
flame is incised upon the martyred air   ;
the city dissolves in foaming craters, stars
falling in multitudes dazzle the sky with fire,
and I pursue them, I am pursued, and
they are everywhere.

Now there is no more brightness, and no shadow
but the shadow of a thought, and I'm in jail enough
to know conviction with prisoner certainty,
haunted by protest, lacking completion's proof
surrounded by shadows
more plausible than love.

BURLESQUE

Up in the second balcony
the dark man's hand moves at his thigh,
he turns congested eyes to floor.
The crowd still stamps and brays for more   :

Magenta flares strip grace away
peeling attraction down to this   :
thighs' alternation, shrugging breasts,
silk tapping the mons veneris   ;

The adequate trough inclines and dips
rising venereally to view   :
stained by the shifting light to blue,
the pearl scarf simmers at her hips.

With each contraction of desire
the appealing flesh is whipped entire,
ambushed in spasms.
                        In the street,
   the raw light serves as index to
   upturning avid faces who
   shine all the signals of defeat.

An army of horns moves up the hall,
drums hurry to their crisis where
awkward in fear, the audience
at last confronts a dancer bare   :
these naked multitudes exposed to her   :
   bright shoulders, glossy length of leg,
   the lapsing beat persists, to beg
salving of lives of these thighs' stir.

We are drenched in confusion, drowning among lights
that flare across stormed waters   showing here
the faces pitiable with hesitation,

eyes groaning past the corpse's sneer,
the twisted words of all the unlucky, spent
on brightened flesh of these impossible dear　　:

The blemished faces and impeccable thighs
are those we paint with lights to make us wise,
consigning our total beauty now to this　　:
the clutching loins and intolerable kiss.

M O V I E

Spotlight her face   her face has no light in it
touch the cheek with light   inform the eyes
press meanings on those lips.
                              See cities from the air,
fix a cloud in the sky, one bird in the bright air,
one perfect mechanical flower in her hair.

Make your young men ride over the mesquite plains   ;
produce our country on film   :   here are the flaming shrubs,
the Negroes put up their hands in Hallelujahs,
the young men balance at the penthouse door.
We focus on the screen   :   look   they tell us
you are a nation of similar whores   remember the Maine
remember you have a democracy of champagne   —

And slowly the female face kisses the young man,
over his face the twelve-foot female head
the yard-long mouth enlarges and yawns
                              The End

Here is a city   here the village grows
here are the rich men standing rows on rows,
but the crowd seeps behind the cowboy the lover the king,
past the constructed sets America rises
the bevelled classic doorways   the alleys of trees are witness
America rises in a wave a mass
pushing away the rot.

                The Director cries Cut!
hoarsely CUT   and the people send pistons of force
crashing against the CUT! CUT! of the straw men.

Light is superfluous upon these eyes,
across our minds push new portents of strength
destroying the sets, the flat faces, the mock skies.

METAPHOR TO ACTION

Whether it is a speaker, taut on a platform,
who battles a crowd with the hammers of his words,
whether it is the crash of lips on lips
after absence and wanting   :   we must close
the circuits of ideas, now generate,
that leap in the body's action or the mind's repose.

Over us is a striking on the walls of the sky,
here are the dynamos, steel-black, harboring flame,
here is the man night-walking who derives
tomorrow's manifestoes from this midnight's meeting   ;
here we require the proof in solidarity,
iron on iron, body on body, and the large single beating.

And behind us in time are the men who second us
as we continue.   And near us is our love   :
no forced contempt, no refusal in dogma, the close
of the circuit in a fierce dazzle of purity.
And over us is night a field of pansies unfolding,
charging with heat its softness in a symbol
to weld and prepare for action our minds' intensity.

CITATION FOR HORACE GREGORY

These are our brave, these with their hands in on the work,
hammering out beauty upon the painful stone
turning their grave heads passionately finding
truth and alone and each day subtly slain
and each day born.
                    Revolves
a measured system, world upon world, stemmed fires
and regulated galaxies behind the flattened head,
behind the immortal skull, ticking eternity
in blood and the symbols of living.

The brass voice speaks in the street
                    STRIKE   STRIKE
        the nervous fingers continue elaborately
        drawing consciousness, examining, doing.
Rise to a billboard world of Chesterfields,
Mae West hip-wriggles, Tarzan prowess, the little
nibbling and despicable minds.
                            Here, gentlemen,
here is our gallery of poets   :
                            Jeffers,
a long and tragic drum-roll beating anger,
sick of a catapulting nightmare world,
Eliot, who led us to the precipice
subtly and perfectly   ;   there striking an attitude
rigid and ageing on the penultimate step,
the thoughtful man MacLeish who bent his head
feeling the weight of the living; bent, and turned
the grave important face round to the dead.

And on your left, ladies and gentlemen   :   poets.

Young poets and makers, solve your anguish, see
the brave unmedalled, who dares to shape his mind,

printed with dignity, to the machines of change.
A procession of poets adds one footbeat to the
implacable metric line   :   the great and unbetrayed
    after the sunlight and the failing yellow,
    after the lips bitten with passion and
    gentle, after the deaths, below
    dance-floors of celebration   we turn   we turn
these braveries are permanent.   These gifts
flare on our lives, clarifying, revealed.

We are too young to see our funerals
in pantomime nightly before uneasy beds,
too near beginnings for this hesitation
obliterated in death or carnival.
Deep into time extend the impersonal stairs,
    established barricades will stand,
before they die the brave have set their hand
on rich particular beauty for their heirs.

CATS AND A COCK

for Eleanor Clark

What hill can ever hold us?
                    Standing high
we saw December packed, snow upon snow,
empty until the cars, leaping in beams below,
opened the shadow of the trees in fans
enormous on the plain, fragile and magnified.
Print of the delicate branch sweeping our feet
in hundred hugeness, passing to white again.

Up the dark hill a pack of cats   :
bursting from hollows, streaming to the crest,
streaming all night toward dawn
when green invaded east.
We stood to hear the rigid cock cry Five
a black cock crowing over cold water,
when all those cats found their sole proud objective
and whirled away to slaughter.

             .   .   .   .   .

                    We walk the streets
                    of the dark city,
                    placards at back
                    light in our heads,

                    Moon rides over us
                    town streams below   :
                    Strike and support us
                    the strike-songs go.

                    Ceilings of stars
                    disturb our faces,
                    tantrums of light
                    summon our eyes;

The daystar stands
hungry for day   :
we file, regarding
this twin morning.

Shall that bind us,
parade and planet,
mobile and point?
No, not yet,

there is a labor
before reunion.
Poets, pickets,
prepare for dawn!

.   .   .   .   .

Come chop the days
lop off the moving hours,
we had not known there were disparate things.

Forget these syntheses and fade
peerless and distant into a distant grave
still hoping unity indeed be made?

I wish you to be saved . . . you wish . . . he wishes . . . she . . .
in conjugation of a destiny.
We were figures rubbed by wind passing upon a frieze,
galloping figures at a column's base
hungrily running from death and marble space.

I give you cats   :   I give you a cock on a hill   :
these stream in beauty   :   that stands blocked in pride
I pledge you death until
they fight and acquiesce, or one has died.

Earnestly and slowly I continue   :
no one could guess how the impact of a word
heard plain and plainly understood
can have attacked us so and so deferred.

Fight them down, deliver yourself, friend!
see, we all fight it down   :   poetry, picket-line,
to master pride and muscle fluid with sun,
conflicting graces moving to one end.

.   .   .   .   .

Witness the unfailing war, season with season,
license and principle, sex with tortured sex,
class versus class, and help us to survey
this city for faces, this hill for tracks.

Sickness will bind itself upon our tissue
clipping off with restriction blood and heat and milk,
becoming real against all disbelief
a sly ghost coughing to advertise its bulk.

Climax to Egypt, our milestone pyramid
forces out history and we remember
conflict of thousands of April processions,
rival winds ripping at the heart's deep chamber.

No natural poison   :   a vicious, banker's thrust
nudges toward dissolution during war,
this peak of open battle points disgust
of decay, counterattacks backing us to our door.

This is when death thrives in the rot
and formal nightmare, zebra of sleep,
presents us madness, diffusion to remember,
to cherish, loss if we lose; and dust to keep.

Resent the nightmare, assume a waking stance,
this clock revolt, held in the hand and striking,
clapping, the violent wings of a struck bird,
speaks your top hour, marks your fatal chance.

.   .   .   .   .

"Still elegiac!   :   between two battles, when one is happy to be
alive !"   —   Rosa Luxemburg

Here was a battle forced by the brain's fortitude,
mapping machines of peace before crisis had come;
and by this planning we create a world
new-hearted, secure from common delirium.

If the strike was won, the prisoners freed at last,
the cataract tapped for power, parade-songs sung   :
Prepare for continuance, open your brilliant love,
your life,   —   front April, give it tongue   !

.   .   .   .   .

Below the flowering hedge
rest in the light, forget
grief's awful violet
and indecision's wedge
driven into your pride,
and how the past has died.

Here is transition   :
pain, but no surgeon's knife
:   anaesthetize your life?
you lose the vision
of how you simply walk
toward a younger folk,

simply, a flaming wire
advancing on the night,
reducing midnight
to clear noon-fire   ;
moving upon the future
and large, clean stature
nearer to all your nature.

.   .   .   .   .

The latchpieces of consciousness unfasten.
We are stroked out of dream and night and myth,
and turning slowly to awareness, listen
to the soft bronchial whisperings of death.

Never forget in legendary darkness
the ways of the hands' turning and the mouth's ways,
wander in the fields of change and not remember
a voice and many voices and the evening's burning.

Turn and remember, this is the world made plain
by chart and signal, instrument and name   :

to some we say Master, others call Sister,
to some we offer nothing but love   :

flier in advance, the cloud over his mouth   ;
the inventor who produces the moment of proof   ;
a sun and moon and other several stars   ;
and those who know each other over wars.

Cats stream upon a hill,
the poet-cock breaks his throat now to say   :
Moment of Proof, May dawn transposing night,
partisan dawn's on the side of day!

    .   .   .   .   .

What hill can ever hold us?
                        Deeply night
found you intent upon this city river,
asleep at heart (turn light to her at last,
it shall be to her
as wellwater)   :
going all day along the gilded air
you saw at midnight
(going, down to the river, haunted by fog-horns) :
steam escaping over the spouting manhole,
a rout of white cats racing through the street.
Wet street, and the fight was ended there,
cats and that cock, fearful antagonists
resolved in fog, a quick pack running uphill
to a cock rigid with joy; running, but not to kill.

    .   .   .   .   .

"Forehead to forehead I meet thee, this third time, Moby Dick!"   —
                      Herman Melville

Moment of proof, when the body holds its vision,
masses recognize masses, knowledge without all end   ;
face fathoms other face, all the hills open sunrise,
mouth sets on mouth   ;   Spring, and the tulips
              totter in the wind.

Forfeit in love, forfeit in conflict, here
met and at last marked clear in principle,
desire meets desire, the chase expands, and now
forever we course, knowing the marks of growth,
               seeing the signals.

Now we remember winter-tormented cities,
the August farm's overgrown hollow, thick with goldenrod,
the impetus of strain, and places where
love set its terminals, the vivid hunger
               and satisfying food.

Mayday is moment of proof, when recognition
binds us in protest, binds us under a sun
of love and subtle thought and the ductile wish.
Tomorrow's Mayday.   ——   How many are we?
             We'll be everyone.

No hill can ever hold us, peak enlists peak,
climax forces out climax, proud cock, cats streaming,
poets and pickets contriving a valid country,
  : Mayday moment, forever provoking new
             belief and blooming.

THE BLOOD IS JUSTIFIED

Beat out continuance in the choking veins
before emotion betrays us, and we find
staring behind our faces, accomplices of death.
Not to die, but slowly to validate our lives   :
simply to move, lightly burdened, alone,
carrying in this brain survival, carrying
within these ribs, history,
the past deep in the bone.

    Unthread time till its empty needle prick your flesh
    sewing your scars with air, treating the wounds
    only by laceration   and the blood is fresh
    blood on our skin on our lips over our eyes.

Living they move on a canvas of centuries
restored from death in artful poses, found
once more by us, descendants, foraging,
ravelling time back over American ground.
How did they wish, grandparents of these wars,
what cataracts of ambition fell across their brains?   :

The heavy boots kicked stones down Wisconsin roads,
Augusta Coller danced her début at Oshkosh   :
they spoke these names   :   Milwaukee, Waukesha,
the crackle and drawl of Indian strange words.

    Jungle-savage the south
    raw green and shining branches, the crying
    of parakeets, the pointed stone,
    the altars stained with oil   :
    Mexico   :   and Canada wheaten and polar with
    snow halfway up the sky   :
    all these unknown.

: What treason to their race has fathered us?
    They walked in the towns, the men selling clothing etc.
    the women tatting and boiling down grape jelly.
: If they were asked this, surely they did not answer.

Over the country, Wisconsin, Chicago, Yonkers,
I was begotten, American branch no less because
I call on the great names of other countries.
I do not say   :   Forgive, to my kindred dead,
only   :   Understand my treason, See I betray you kissing,
I overthrow your milestones weeping among your tombs.

From out your knowing eyes I sprang, child of your distant wombs,
of your full lips.   Speaking allegiance, I turn,
steadfastly to destroy your hope.   Your cargo in me
swings to ports hostile to your old intent.

In us recurrences.   :   My generation feeds
the wise assault on your anticipation,
repeating historic sunderings, betraying our fathers,
all parricidal in our destinies.

How much are we American?   Not knowing
those other lands, being
blood wrung from your bone, our pioneers,
we call kindred to you, we claim links, speaking
your tongue, although we pass, shaking
your dream with revolution since we must.
By these roads shall we come upon our country.
Pillowed upon this birthright, we may wake
strong for such treason, brave with your fallen dust.

O, we are afflicted with these present evils,
they press between the mirror and our eyes,
obscuring your loaned mouths and borrowed hair.
We focus on our times, destroying you, fathers
in the long ground   :   you have given strange birth
to us who turn against you in our blood
needing to move in our integrity, accomplices
of life in revolution, though the past
be sweet with your tall shadows, and although
we turn from treasons, we shall accomplish these.

PUBLISHER'S NOTE

The Yale Series of Younger Poets is designed to afford a publishing medium for the work of young men and women who have not yet secured a wide public recognition. It will include only such verse as seems to give the fairest promise for the future of American poetry—to the development of which it is hoped that the Series may prove a stimulus. Communications concerning manuscripts should be addressed to the Editor of The Yale Series of Younger Poets, in care of the Yale University Press, New Haven, Connecticut.

VOLUMES ALREADY ISSUED